Find Freedom

ROMANS

New Community Bible Study Series

BILL HYBELS

WITH KEVIN & SHERRY HARNEY

New Community
KNOWING. LOVING. SERVING. CELEBRATING.

Find
Freedom

ROMANS

ZondervanPublishingHouse

Grand Rapids, Michigan

A Division of HarperCollins*Publishers*

Romans: Find Freedom
Copyright © 1999 by the Willow Creek Association

Requests for information should be addressed to:

ZondervanPublishingHouse
Grand Rapids, Michigan 49530

ISBN: 0-310-22765-8

Interior design by Sherri Hoffman

Printed in the United States of America

03 04 /❖ EP/ 10 9 8 7 6 5

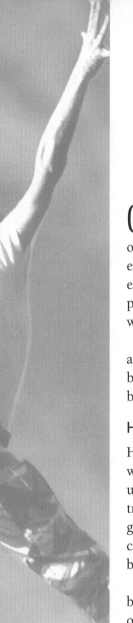

God has created us for community. This need is built into the very fiber of our being, the DNA of our spirit. As Christians, our deepest desire is to see the truth of God's Word as it influences our relationship with others. We long for a dynamic encounter with God's Word, intimate closeness with His people, and radical transformation of our lives. But how can we accomplish those three difficult tasks?

The New Community Bible Study Series creates a place for all of this to happen. In-depth Bible study, community-building opportunities, and life-changing applications are all built into every session of this small group study guide.

How to Build Community

How do we build a strong, healthy Christian community? The whole concept for this study grows out of a fundamental understanding of Christian community that is dynamic and transformational. We believe that Christians don't simply gather to exchange doctrinal affirmations. Rather, believers are called by God to get into each other's lives. We are family, for better or for worse, and we need to connect with each other.

Community is not built through sitting in the same building and singing the same songs. It is forged in the fires of life. When we know each other deeply—the good, the bad, and the ugly—community is experienced. Community grows when we learn to rejoice with one another, celebrating life. Roots grow deep when we know we are loved by others and are free to extend love to them as well. Finally, community deepens and is built when we commit to serve each other and let others serve us. This process of doing ministry and humbly receiving the ministry of others is critical for healthy community life.

Build Community Through Knowing and Being Known

We all long to know others deeply and to be fully known by them. Although we might run from this level of intimacy at times, we all want to have people in our lives who trust us enough to disclose the deep and tender parts of themselves. In turn, we want to reveal some of our feelings, expressing them freely to people we trust.

The first section of each of these six studies creates a place for deep knowing and being known. Through serious reflection on the truth of Scripture, you will be invited to communicate parts of your heart and life with your small group members. You might even discover yourself opening parts of your heart that you have thus far kept hidden. The Bible study and discussion questions do not encourage surface conversation. The only way to go deep in knowing others and being known by them is to dig deep, and this takes some work. Knowing others also takes trust—that you will honor each other and respect each other's confidences.

Build Community Through Celebrating and Being Celebrated

If you have not had a good blush recently, read a short book in the Bible called Song of Songs. It's a record of a bride and groom writing poetic and romantic love letters to each other. They are freely celebrating every conceivable aspect of each other's personality, character, and physical appearance. At one point the groom says, "You have made my heart beat fast with a single glance from your eyes." Song of Songs is a reckless celebration of life, love, and all that is good.

We need to recapture the joy and freedom of celebration. In every session of this study, your group will commit to celebrate together. Although there are many ways to express joy, we will let our expression of celebration come through prayer. In each session you will take time to come before the God of joy and celebrate who He is and what He is doing. You will also have opportunity to celebrate what God is doing in your life and the lives of those who are a part of your small group. You will become a community of affirmation, celebration, and joy through your prayer time together.

You will need to be sensitive during this time of prayer together. Not everyone feels comfortable praying with a group of people. Be aware that each person is starting at a different place in their freedom to pray in a group, and be patient. Seek to promote a warm and welcoming atmosphere where each person can stretch a little and learn what it means to be a community that celebrates with God in the center.

Build Community Through Loving and Being Loved

Unless we are exchanging deeply committed levels of love with a few people, we will die slowly on the inside. This is precisely why so many people feel almost nothing at all. If we don't learn to exchange love with family and friends, we will eventually grow numb and no longer believe love is even a possibility. This is not God's plan. He hungers for us to be loved and to give love to others. As a matter of fact, He wants this for us even more than we want it for ourselves.

Every session in this study will address the area of loving and being loved. You will be challenged, in your personal life and as a small group, to be intentional and consistent about building love relationships. You will get practical tools and be encouraged to set measurable goals for giving and receiving love.

Build Community Through Serving and Being Served

Community is about serving and humbly allowing others to serve you. The single most stirring example of this is recorded in John 13, where Jesus takes the position of the lowest servant and washes the feet of His followers. He gives them a powerful example and then calls them to follow. Servanthood is at the very core of community. To sustain deep relationships over a long period of time, there must be humility and a willingness to serve each other.

At the close of each session will be a clear challenge to servanthood. As a group, and as individual followers of Christ, you will discover that community is built through serving others. You will also find that your own small group members will grow in their ability to extend service to your life.

Bible Study Basics

To get the most out of this study, you will need to prepare and participate. Here are some guidelines to help you.

Preparing for the Study

1. If possible, even if you are not the leader, look over each lesson before you meet, read the Bible passages, and answer the questions. The more you are prepared, the more you will gain from the study.
2. Begin your preparation time with prayer. Ask God to help you understand the passage and apply it to your life.
3. A good modern translation, such as the New International Version, the New American Standard Bible, or the New Revised Standard Version, will give you the most help. Questions in this guide are based on the New International Version.
4. Read and reread the passages. You must know what the passage says before you can understand what it means and how it applies to you.
5. Write your answers in the spaces provided in the study guide. This will help you to participate more fully in the discussion, and will also help you personalize what you are learning.
6. Keep a Bible dictionary handy to look up unfamiliar words, names, or places.

Participating in the Study

1. Be willing to join in the discussion. The leader of the group will not be lecturing but will encourage people to discuss what they have learned in the passage. Plan to share what God has taught you during your preparation time.
2. Stick to the passages being studied. Base your answers on the verses being discussed rather than on outside authorities such as commentaries or your favorite author or speaker.

3. Try to be sensitive to the other members of the group. Listen attentively when they speak, and be affirming whenever you can. This will encourage more hesitant members of the group to participate.
4. Be careful not to dominate the discussion. By all means participate, but allow others to have equal time.
5. If you are a discussion leader or a participant who wants further insights, you will find additional comments in the Leader's Notes at the back of this book.

Romans—Find Freedom

Freedom!

The word inspires the hearts of countless people around the world. Those who are in bondage or slavery long for freedom like a starving man hungers for food. They dream of a day when the shackles will be broken. They hope for a time when they will be on equal footing with those around them. Having suffered in captivity, they yearn for the day when they will be set free.

Those who already have freedom know how precious it is, and are willing to defend it with their lives. If one nation threatens another nation's freedom, citizens will take up arms, and armies will march. Freedom is never surrendered easily, without a fight.

The book of Romans proclaims freedom to all who are enslaved and hope to the hopeless. In Romans, God announces that every prisoner can be set free and every slave liberated. Yet Paul is not writing of political freedom, but spiritual freedom. This is freedom that will last a lifetime, freedom that can never be taken away, freedom that brings life where there was once death.

If you long for a freedom that will bring you limitless power, forgiveness of sins, hope for the future, rich community with others, and a purpose for life, look no further than the book of Romans. It is all here. Dig in and discover freedom like you have never experienced before.

The Best of the Best

Martin Luther called the letter to the church at Rome the "chief part of the New Testament and the purest gospel." Another writer refers to the book of Romans as the "cathedral of the Christian faith." Many theologians have said that if they had to spend the rest of their lives on a deserted island with

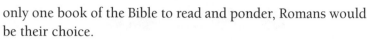

only one book of the Bible to read and ponder, Romans would be their choice.

The book of Romans is absolutely packed. When we open this powerful book of the Bible, it can be like standing at the base of Mount Everest, looking up and feeling overwhelmed by its grandeur and magnitude. Yet, at the same time, we are strangely attracted to the challenge of scaling its great heights and seeing the world from a whole new vantage point.

If you are able to get the basics of this book under your belt, I don't think you will ever be the same. The contents and subject matter are so expansive that any serious study will bring powerful transformation to your life.

Paul and the Roman Church

The apostle Paul was not the founding pastor of the church in Rome. As a matter of fact, he was not a pastor there at all, and at the time he wrote this letter, Paul had never actually been to Rome. He had longed to go there many times, but it had never worked out. Many of the people in Rome had heard of him, but to some, he was still a stranger. Yet out of love for these believers he had never met, Paul wrote to the church, bringing a message of freedom, hope, and vision.

As you study this powerful book of the Bible, invite the Holy Spirit of God to set you free in new and amazing ways. Pray for a clear vision for what the church, the bride of Jesus, could be. Allow God's power and presence to fill and transform your life. You will be amazed at what He will do!

An Urgent Message to the World

ROMANS 1

A young boy comes running into the house and yells, "Dad, Mom, hurry! I need help!"

A mother gets a phone call in the middle of the day from the principal. "Come to the office right away. It's urgent!"

A father pulls his car into the garage after a long day of work. His wife's car is not in the garage, and the house is strangely quiet. He spots a note on the table in his wife's handwriting, but the letters are poorly formed and pressed deeply into the paper. "Meet us at the emergency room at the hospital as soon as you can get there."

It's urgent! It's important! No time to waste!

We have all experienced moments when someone came to us with a sense of urgency. They needed help *now!* Their tone of voice, the volume of their words, the look in their eyes, the intensity of their gestures—all of these made it clear that they were urgent about what they were saying.

Making the Connection

1. Describe a time that someone came to you with a real sense of urgency. How did you respond to their news or request?

Knowing and Being Known

Read Romans 1:1–17

Still Urgent After All These Years

I attended a conference of itinerant evangelists from over 130 countries in Amsterdam. Billy Graham expressed the consensus opinion of the thousands of people attending there: "The greatest need of the hour is the revival of the Church of Jesus Christ." We all joined together at this conference to make the following dedication to the ministry commissioned by Jesus:

We affirm our commitment to the Great Commission of our Lord and declare our willingness to go anywhere, do anything, and sacrifice anything God requires of us in the fulfillment of that commission.

As I look out on the world scene today, I am absolutely convinced that a revival among the people of God would spill over in blessing to the millions without Christ, resulting in hundreds of thousands of lost, alienated, hopeless people being brought to the Savior.

—LeRoy Eims, *Laboring in the Harvest* (NavPress, 1985, p. 11)

The urgency of bringing the message of Jesus Christ to the ends of the earth has never changed. His Great Commission is the same today as it was when Jesus first spoke these words two thousand years ago:

"All authority in heaven and on earth has been given to me. Therefore go and make disciples of all nations, baptizing them in the name of the Father and of the Son and of the Holy Spirit, and teaching them to obey everything I have commanded you. And surely I am with you always, to the very end of the age."

(Matthew 28:18–20)

2. What are some of the things Paul writes to show his urgency about his message to the church in Rome (vv. 9–11, 15–16)?

   What are some of the behaviors in your life that show you are urgent about the message of Jesus Christ?

3. The urgency of Paul's message revolved around who Jesus is and what He has done. According to this passage, who is Jesus Christ (vv. 3–4, 9)?

   According to Paul's teaching in this passage, what has Jesus done (vv. 4–6, 16–17)?

4. How did Paul feel about the people in the church in Rome (vv. 6–15)?

How do you feel about the people who are part of your church?

What do you do to show the depth of your feelings for other followers of Christ?

Read Romans 1:18–23

No More Excuses

Romans 1:18–23, just six short verses, has the potential to make us very uncomfortable. Paul was deeply urgent about spreading the message of Jesus Christ in Rome and anywhere else he could go. The driving force of this urgency was his awareness that unbelievers everywhere were daily committing a spiritual crime so heinous that God's wrath would be poured out on them on Judgment Day. Paul was so upset at the thought of these unbelievers suffering in hell for eternity that he could not conceal his grief.

5. Paul clearly taught that God reveals Himself through the things He has made. How have you seen and experienced the glory of God through His creation?

How is this kind of revelation universal and available to all people?

6. What is the crime or sin that people commit against God that leads to their condemnation (vv. 21–23)?

7. What are examples today of how people do *one* of the following:

   - Fail to give God glory.
   - Refuse to give thanks to God.
   - Grow futile in their thinking.
   - Claim to be wise when they are fools.
   - Worship idols and images rather than God.

The Toughest Thing a Parent Could Ever Do

Some parents have had to make the heartbreaking decision to let their teenage child go to follow a path that is dangerous and sometimes even self-destructive. With deep grief, they recognize that their own child has become rebellious, recalcitrant, and destructive, and after years of exercising patience and kindness, finally they have to say, "Go! You have wanted to break free from our family and every value we hold dear. We give you that freedom. Have it your way. Leave!"

Parents never take joy in that moment, but instead feel sorrow and a deep desire for the child to come home. But the parents know that their child must be released. With a broken heart, loving parents give their child over to his or her own desires and rebellion.

8. Three times the apostle Paul tells of God giving His children over to their own sinful desires. Each of the three cycles seems to spiral deeper and deeper into sin and lead the children farther and farther from their heavenly Father. What are the sins the children of God entered into each time God gave them over to their own desires?

    • (vv. 24–25) God gave them over to . . .

    • (vv. 26–27) God gave them over to . . .

    • (vv. 28–31) God gave them over to . . .

How have you seen this same downward spiral in the lives of those who are running from God today?

9. If God is truly a loving heavenly Father, why would He ever let His children go?

10. Paul ends this section by saying, "Although they know God's righteous decree that those who do such things deserve death, they not only continue to do these very things but also approve of those who practice them" (v. 32). How is this attitude reflected in our world today?

How can we refuse to affirm the things that break God's heart?

Celebrating and Being Celebrated

Do you know of anyone who has had a rebellious child who repented and returned? Take time as a group to praise God for the healing in this family.

Then celebrate how God has welcomed you home with open arms when you have run away from Him. Pray together and give thanks to God for offering you complete forgiveness for all the sins you have committed in rebellion toward Him.

Serving and Being Served

Identify one couple in your church who has gone through the gut-wrenching, heartbreaking process of letting their child go. Commit as a group to pray for the parents and the son or daughter. Ask a group member to contact the family and let them know that you will be praying for their son or daughter and for their strained relationship. Also, ask if there is anything you can do to uphold them through the pain and turmoil of this time.

Loving and Being Loved

Imagine a groom on his wedding day. He has waited and waited to see his bride, and now there she is. She stands at the end of the aisle: beautiful, radiant, beaming! His heart almost bursts as he sees her walking toward him. She is his bride!

This is just the slightest glimpse of how Jesus sees His church, His bride.

I think it is fair to say that we can measure our love for Jesus Christ by measuring our love for His church. How often do you sincerely thank God for the beauty and power of gathered worship? When was the last time you were overwhelmed by the power of the church to reach out and impact the world? Do you find deep joy in being together in community with other followers of Christ? Do you feel like something essential and crucial is missing in your life when you can't gather with God's people for a period of time? Does your heart race when you think of the church, the bride of Christ?

Talk as a group about how you can express love for the church, Christ's bride. What is one thing you can do to help strengthen and build up your church?

How to Find Forgiveness for Moral Failures

ROMANS 3

Have you ever experienced a church split? Maybe you have been part of a split or maybe you know someone who has walked this gut-wrenching, heartbreaking path. Those who have been through a church split never forget it.

Some churches split over doctrinal issues, some over budgetary decisions, some over personality or philosophical issues. No matter what causes the division, the pain is still the same. Family members fight, friendships are shattered, children draw lines against parents, and the body of Christ ends up crippled.

Factions form, and leaders emerge on both sides of the issue. With time, one faction sits on one side of the aisle and the opposing faction on the other side, with the center aisle of the church becoming the demilitarized zone. During sermons on love, people glare across the aisle at each other. During worship, the focus is no longer on God and His glory, but on the battle. People who used to share the communion elements or be part of a small group with each other are now enemies.

The rumors begin to grow and circulate. Accusations are hurled. Secret meetings are held. Ministries suffer. Visitors come and never return because they can feel the tension among the people. As things get ugly, people begin to manipulate the church by withholding their giving or refusing to serve.

The beautiful bride of Jesus Christ is defaced, molested, and abused. With time, all that is left of a once vibrant witness and community of Christ followers is attractive real estate, some nice buildings, and a remnant of wounded people who dream of a better time and days gone by.

Making the Connection

1. Have you or someone close to you ever been through a church split or a serious division? If so, how does this kind of experience impact a follower of Christ?

Knowing and Being Known

Read Romans 3:9–20

But What Is Sin?

Saint Paul reminds us, we are not our own (1 Cor. 6:19). We belong entirely to Christ.... Our thoughts, our actions, our desires, are by rights more his than our own. But we have to struggle to ensure that God always receives from us what we owe him by right. If we do not labor to overcome our natural weakness, our disordered and selfish passions, what belongs to God in us will be withdrawn from the sanctifying power of his love and will be corrupted by selfishness, blinded by irrational desire, hardened by pride, and will eventually plunge into the abyss of moral nonentity which is called sin.

Sin is the refusal of spiritual life, the rejection of the inner order and peace that come from our union with the divine will. In a word, sin is the refusal of God's will and of his love. It is not only a refusal to "do" this or that thing willed by God, or a determination to do what he forbids. It is more radically a refusal to be what we are, a rejection of our mysterious, contingent, spiritual reality hidden in the very mystery of God. Sin is our refusal to be what we were created to be—sons of God, images of God. Ultimately sin, while seeming to be an assertion of freedom, is a flight from the freedom and the responsibility of divine sonship."

—Thomas Merton, *Life and Holiness* (Abbey of Gethsemani, Inc., 1963)

2. How are all human beings portrayed in this passage?

   What would this powerful portrayal of the human condition have said to both the Jews and the Gentiles (people on both sides of the aisle)?

3. Paul quotes numerous Old Testament passages which teach about the human condition without God (3:10–18). What would Paul say to a person who might make *one* of the following statements:

   • I've been a pretty good person; I'm sure God is happy with my life.
   • Well, I know I've done a few wrong things, but I'm a lot better person than most of my friends and colleagues at work.
   • I am certain God is pleased with me. I attend church weekly, put a little money in the offering plate, and have remained faithful to my spouse. What else could God expect from me?

4. What can the law accomplish (3:19–20)?

What is the law not able to accomplish?

What is the purpose and function of the law?

5. In light of all Paul says about the human heart and condition, where will we end up without God in *one* of the following areas:

    - What will a marriage look like without God's presence and help?
    - What will a government look like if it rejects God's ways?
    - What will friendships be based on without Christ in the center of them?
    - What will business practices and ethics look like if God is expelled from the marketplace?
    - What will a church community look like if God's ways are sacrificed for personal agendas?

The All World Hall of Fame

Imagine that a very wealthy group of baseball fanatics gets together and decides that the Baseball Hall of Fame is accepting too many players. This group believes the standards are way too low and that someone has to raise the bar, so they form a new organization called the "All World Baseball Hall of Fame." They commit to give $25,000 cash to every person who is accepted into *their* Hall of Fame. They will also give each player a mansion in Florida and many other perks and prizes.

Once they have established the benefits of being in their Hall of Fame, they set out three clear requirements for all those who will make it into their exclusive club. First, they must have played major league ball for five seasons. Second, they cannot have made a single error in their entire career—no throwing errors, no fielding errors, no wild pitches, no stolen bases, no errors of any kind. The third and final requirement is that each player must bat one thousand. There is no room for a fly-out, strikeout, fielder's choice, or any other mistake at the plate.

If a player could do it, what great benefits he would experience! But think about it. What are the odds? It is almost unheard of for a player to go *one season* without an error, much less five seasons in a row. It has never happened! The batting average record was set in 1894 by Hugh Duffy at .438. That same season he committed twenty-seven errors. Even the best batting record in history is still not even halfway to the standard of perfection.

The hard reality is, the standard set by this group of wealthy visionaries is impossible to reach. The idea of getting into the "All World Hall of Fame" is appealing, but no one will ever make it.

6. Like the baseball player who realizes that five perfect seasons is impossible to accomplish, we stand before a holy God and His perfect law and have to confess, "I can't measure up. I can't deal with my own sins. I can't make it on my own." What has God done to make it possible for us to measure up, find forgiveness from our sins, and make it into heaven (3:21–26)?

7. Describe when you first realized the price God paid to offer you forgiveness of sins.

   How does this reality impact the way you live your life today?

8. How does the sacrifice and shed blood of Jesus (3:25) satisfy God's demand for justice?

   When you reflect on the reality that Jesus paid the price of His own blood and life so that you could be forgiven of your sins, how does it make you feel?

Read Romans 3:27–31

That Confusing Thing Called Humility

Where once pride was recognized as a fatal flaw, in our day it comes close to being celebrated. We live in what Christopher Lasch has called "the Culture of Narcissism." Muhammad Ali's signature line expressed the quest of the rest of us: "I am the greatest." Boxing promoter Don King was quoted in the *Los Angeles Times* as saying, "I never cease to amaze my own self"—and then added, "I say that humbly." How would that come out if he were to say it with pride?

In the place of pride, Jesus invites us to a life of humility: "All who humble themselves will be exalted." But we have become badly confused about humility.... Humility has to do with submitted willingness. It involves a healthy self-forgetfulness. We will know we have begun to make progress in humility when we find that we get so enabled by the Holy Spirit to live in the moment that we cease to be preoccupied with ourselves.

—John Ortberg, *The Life You've Always Wanted*
(Zondervan, 1997, pp. 101–102)

9. When people in the church understand their own sinfulness, the price God has paid, and the forgiveness they can experience through Jesus, everything should change. Choose one of the following attitudes and discuss what can happen when we become profoundly aware of what God has done for us:

- Boasting and bragging about our spiritual status (v. 27).
- Believing we have to keep every aspect of the law or God won't love us (v. 28).
- Conflicting attitudes between factions in a church (vv. 29–30).
- Believing we can disregard the law of God and do whatever we want (v. 31).

10. Without using a name, describe a relationship you have with another follower of Christ that has become strained or has been broken.

What is one thing you can do to begin to restore this relationship and to seek reconciliation?

How can your small group members pray for you and encourage you as you seek healing with this person?

Celebrating and Being Celebrated

As a group, pray for healing in relationships that have become strained. If you are standing on the other side of the aisle from a brother or sister in Christ and are refusing to seek reconciliation, ask your group members to pray for you to find courage to take steps toward healing in this relationship. If you are at a point where you have no desire to reconcile, you might need to begin by having your small group members pray for a softening of your heart. Praise God and thank Him for offering the power and possibility of healed relationships.

Serving and Being Served

Paul paints a sobering picture of the human heart and condition without God. Without God's working and without followers of Christ actively involved, any organization or institution will begin to disintegrate. Talk as a group about practical ways you can bring the healing influence of Christ to organizations in your community, to your schools, to your state government, and even to national organizations and institutions.

Loving and Being Loved

Take time in the coming week for personal introspection. Ask the Holy Spirit to show you one relationship where pride and boasting exist. Confess your pride to God and pray for Him to humble you in this relationship. Seek to show God's love to this person by offering some act of service that would demand genuine humility on your part. You might want to have a small group member praying you through this new territory.

Free at Last

ROMANS 6

Many years ago I had an opportunity to explain the gospel to a young man I met during my summer break. By his own admission, he was a frequent user of drugs, entrenched in personal debt, and associated with a group of friends that he described as "a bunch of burnouts and potheads." He was working in an unfulfilling job at minimum wage and saw nothing exciting in his future. He was also clear that he did not see much hope for significant change.

I thought, *Here is a person who will be responsive to the transforming message of the cross and Christ's work on his behalf.* I talked with him about it for a little while, and then asked if he might be interested in meeting with me again some time to talk more about this subject. He said words to the effect, "No, thanks. I enjoy my freedom."

I remember thinking, *How ironic.* As I looked at him, I saw a man in bondage, a broken person in the chains of drugs, indebtedness, and the damaging influence of people who were just as enslaved as he was. It looked to me like he was shackled to a hopeless future with no chance of escape.

Then I stopped and realized that this was exactly how he saw me. He saw me chained to a restrictive religious lifestyle that left no room for fun or self-expression. His perception was that I was enslaved to God and all of the limiting rules and regulations that come with the life of a Christian. In his mind, what could be worse than the life of slavery I was bound to live?

I was struck by the profound irony. He thought he was free and that I was in spiritual chains. I looked at him and thought that he was enslaved and that I was free.

Making the Connection

1. Describe people you have encountered who believed they were truly free, but who were actually enslaved and in bondage.

What caused the immense difference in how you saw them and how they saw themselves?

Knowing and Being Known

Read Romans 6:6, 17, 19–20

Call Sin What It Is

As human beings we tend to give ourselves the benefit of the doubt. We see our sins but want to justify and excuse them. Yet the apostle Paul is clear that we are all slaves to sin outside of Christ. Our sin might manifest itself in gross moral misconduct, or the subtle poison of a prideful and arrogant heart. But we must never forget that all sin offends God. C. S. Lewis, in his book *Mere Christianity,* highlights the deceit of sin:

All the worst pleasures are purely spiritual: the pleasure of putting other people in the wrong, of bossing and patronizing and spoiling sport, and back-biting; the pleasures of power and hatred. For there are two things inside me, competing with the human self which I must try to become. They are the Animal self, and the Diabolical self. The Diabolical self is the worse of the two. That is why a cold, self-righteous prig who goes regularly to church may be far nearer to hell than a prostitute. But of course, it is better to be neither.

—C. S. Lewis, *Mere Christianity* (MacMillan, 1958, pp. 94–95)

2. What was our relationship to sin before Christ entered our life (6:6, 17, 19–20)?

Before you became a follower of Christ, how did you experience the gripping power of sin in your life?

3. What happened in your life to open your eyes to the reality that you were a slave to sin and in need of being set free?

4. What would the apostle Paul say to a nonbeliever who confidently declares, "I am free to do whatever I want. I make my own choices, set my own path, and control my own destiny. I'm free! It's you Christians who are in bondage."

Read Romans 6:1–14

Jesus Gives Us the Upper Hand

God truly carries out his regenerating work in his own people, so that the sway of sin is abolished in them. For the Spirit dispenses a power whereby they might gain the upper hand and become victors in the struggle.... This comes to pass through the mercy of God, so that the saints (all followers of Christ)—otherwise deservedly sinners and guilty before God—are freed from this guilt.

—John Calvin, *Institutes of the Christian Religion*, Book 1
(Westminster Press, 1960, p. 603)

5. How does the apostle Paul use the image of baptism (going down into the water and coming up out of the water) as an image of our changed relationship to sin (6:3–4)?

How does Paul use the image of Jesus' death, burial, and resurrection (6:5–11) as a picture of our changed relationship to sin?

6. Paul is clear that through Christ we are brought from death to life (6:13) and from slavery to freedom (6:6–7). Sin no longer has controlling power in our lives. How have you experienced freedom and transformation in *one* of these areas of your life since becoming a follower of Christ:

    • In the way you care for your physical body
    • In the way you treat those who are different than you
    • In the way you view money and material things
    • In the way you treat family members and friends
    • In some other area of your life

7. Jesus sets us free through His death and resurrection. Yet the process of being free takes time. What are some of the practices or disciplines in your life as a Christ follower that have helped you continue to grow in freedom and be released from slavery to sin?

Slaves of Righteousness

Our position, as Christians, is that we have been "enslaved to righteousness." This does not mean that we admire righteousness, nor that we desire to be righteous; it does not mean that we are attempting to be righteous, or attempting to practice righteousness in our daily life. It includes all of these but has a much wider content. What the apostle says is, that we have become "slaves to righteousness"—nothing less. Not "servants," but "slaves" of righteousness! That means that we have come under the power and control and influence of righteousness. As once we were tyrannized over and ruled by and governed by sin, we are now, we may say, tyrannized over and governed and ruled by righteousness itself.

—D. Martyn Lloyd Jones, *Romans, The New Man, Exposition of Chapter 6* (Zondervan, 1973, p. 225)

8. Paul talks about our body being enslaved to sin and being set free through Christ (vv. 18–19). Reflect on various parts of your physical body and give examples of what slavery to sin might look like and what slavery to righteousness in Christ might look like:

What might the use of this body part look like if you have been set free in Christ and are a slave to righteousness?
Your hands ...
Your eyes ...
Your mouth ...
Your mind ...

What might slavery to sin look like in the way you use this part of your body?
Your hands . . .
Your eyes . . .
Your mouth . . .
Your mind . . .

9. What is one area of your life where you have experienced a whole new freedom since becoming a follower of Christ?

Celebrating and Being Celebrated

Thank God for the freedom from sin that Jesus Christ has brought you. Celebrate that you are no longer slaves to sin, but have been set free. Also thank God for making you slaves of righteousness, and pray for your life to reflect this reality more and more with each passing day.

Serving and Being Served

Once we become slaves of righteousness, sin grows more and more visible. Actions, attitudes, and behaviors that never bothered us now stick out like a sore thumb. Too often followers of Christ begin to disconnect with their friends who are not Christians. The reality of their sinful lifestyle can cause tension and friction.

However, God wants us to be His light in a dark world. He wants us to be salt that makes people thirst for the things of God. And we all know that salt doesn't do any good just sitting in a salt shaker. It needs to be poured out to be effective. This is also true for followers of Christ. We can't impact the lives of others unless we are with them.

Seek opportunities to be with friends and acquaintances who are not followers of Christ. Look at your schedule and see how much time you invest in those who are already part of the family. Then, commit yourself to connect with those who need to know the love of Jesus Christ.

Loving and Being Loved

God paid the ultimate price to show His love for you. He laid down the life of His only Son. In the coming week, write a thank you letter to God expressing your love to Him for setting you free from sin and calling you to righteousness. You may want to read your letter to your small group the next time you meet as an expression of praise to God.

It Will Be Worth It All

ROMANS 8

I became a follower of Christ in my late teenage years at a Bible camp in Wisconsin. I had a very definite point at which I came to receive what Christ had done for me and accepted Jesus as the forgiver of my sins and the leader of my life. I knew something dramatic had happened that was going to change me forever.

As I began to grow as a follower of Christ, the director of the camp began to challenge me about what I was going to do with my life. Once, he pulled me aside to read 2 Peter 3:10: "But the day of the Lord will come like a thief. The heavens will disappear with a roar; the elements will be destroyed by fire, and the earth and everything in it will be laid bare." Wow! He pointed out that when Jesus returns, every single one of my material possessions was going up in smoke. What a comforting thought for a motivated young materialist to ponder.

About this same time in my life, I heard a speaker say that we should put a big red tag with the word *temporary* on every material thing we fall in love with. This would help us remember that none of the stuff of this world is going to last forever. The toys and trinkets of this life are not eternal. We should not get our hearts set on these things.

Another time my camp director pointed me to a passage that says, "Do you not know that in a race all the runners run, but only one gets the prize? Run in such a way as to get the prize" (1 Corinthians 9:24). He reminded me that there are two races I could spend my life running: an earthly race with a prize that will perish and rot, and a heavenly race with an imperishable prize. I remember my camp director looking at me and asking, "Which race are you going to spend your life running?"

Making the Connection

1. Respond to *one* of the following questions:

    - What are some of the "treasures" we can store up that will last forever?
    - If you had to red tag one or two material things as a reminder that they are just temporary, what would you tag and why?
    - What are you doing to condition yourself so that you are in shape to run God's race?

Knowing and Being Known

Read Romans 8:1–17

A Sinister Strategy

In Revelation 12:10, we learn that the Devil is called "the accuser." This passage teaches us that Satan is in the business of accusing God's people *every night* and *every day*. One of Satan's strategies is to take the normal guilt that comes from wrongdoing and intensify and exaggerate it so he can push us to the limits of depression and self-hatred. The Evil One knows that a thoroughly discouraged Christian is an utterly useless Christian.

When a follower of Christ does anything wrong, the Enemy jumps on this opportunity and begins to whisper, "Now you've done it! That was the last straw. God has had it with you! His patience has ended. His grace is used up. He is sick and tired of your sinful mistakes. He is fed up with your premeditated foul-ups and sins." And sometimes, when we are really susceptible, he even tries to tell us, "You are now condemned in the sight of God. No amount of pleading, confession, or repentance will get you out of this one. Don't even bother asking for forgiveness this time. You have crossed the line. There is no hope for you!"

2. What are some of the accusing and condemning tactics the Devil uses to beat down and discourage followers of Christ?

What is one area where the Devil has tried to condemn you?

3. What has God done so that we do not have to live under the condemning accusations of the Devil (vv. 1–5)?

4. Paul is drawing a radical and clear distinction between those who are under the law of sin (non-Christians) and those who are under the law of the Spirit (Christ followers). What does Paul teach about freedom and bondage (vv. 2–3)?

How have you experienced freedom and new life since you became a follower of Jesus Christ?

5. What does Paul teach about mindset and life focus for those under the law of the Spirit as opposed to those under the law of sin (vv. 5–7)?

6. What does Paul teach about obligation and devotion for those under the law of the Spirit as opposed to those under the law of sin (vv. 12–14)?

Read Romans 8:18–30

What Will You Sacrifice?

Through the history of the church there have been many followers of Christ who have been willing to sacrifice everything because they knew that the sufferings of this life were small compared to the glory God has prepared for His children. One such person was Jim Elliot. He went as a missionary to bring the message of God's love to an unreached group of people, and he was killed by them before he was able to tell them about Jesus. In the book *Shadow of the Almighty*, his wife, Elisabeth, tells of Jim's life of faith and her call to go and reach the same tribe of people who had killed her husband.

As you read the reflections from Jim Elliot's personal journal, you will discover the heart of a person willing to give everything up for the sake of following Jesus:

"He is no fool who gives up what he cannot keep to gain what he cannot lose!"

"God, I pray Thee, light these idle sticks of my life and may I burn for Thee. Consume my life, my God, for it is Thine. I seek not a long life, but a full one, like you, Lord Jesus."

"Father, take my life, yea, my blood if thou wilt, and consume it with Thine enveloping fire. I would not save it, for it is not mine to save. Have it Lord, have it all. Pour out my life as an offering for the world. Blood is only of value as it flows before Thine altar."

—Elisabeth Elliot, *The Shadow of the Almighty* (Harper and Row, 1958)

7. Take a moment to write down three ways you have suffered over the past year:

How has God used one of these experiences to refine and mature you?

8. Take a moment to write down three promises you have for *today, tomorrow,* and *eternity* because of Jesus Christ:

    Describe one of these promises and how it brings you joy and strength.

9. How do the promises of God influence the way you view your suffering?

    How can the example of how Jesus faced suffering encourage you in the middle of your times of pain and struggle?

Read Romans 8:31–39

God Is for Us ... He Proved It!

Jesus paid a tremendous price to be with us. Certainly the cross was the most obvious cost. But I believe more is in view.

We focus so much on the fact that Jesus died for us, we sometimes forget that he also lived for us and still lives for us. If Jesus had simply come as himself, and not as one of us, the Bible makes it quite clear that we could not have borne the sight of his presence, any more than Moses could have looked directly at the face of God.

Imagine what it would be like to be at the Father's side one moment and struggling to sleep in a cattle trough the next. Imagine what it would be like to go from hearing the praise of angels to suffering the taunts of stupid men. The cost to Jesus is an indication of the incredible value of what he came to give us. And because no one will ever fully know what that cost Jesus, we can only begin to understand the incredible value of the gift to us.

—Michael Card, *Immanuel: Reflections on the Life of Christ*
(Thomas Nelson, 1990)

10. What has God done to prove His love for you?

How does it make you feel when you realize the depth of love God has for you?

11. What are some of the things that can never separate you from God's love in Jesus Christ?

Why do we need such a clear and powerful reminder that nothing can separate us from God's love?

Celebrating and Being Celebrated

Take time to thank and praise God for never letting you go. Pray through specific times when you have struggled and suffered, and give God thanks for holding on to you every step of the way.

Serving and Being Served

We all have friends or family members who have gone through tough times. Sometimes we pray for them. Sometimes the best thing we can do is help carry their burden. At other times they need us to simply be with them and be a friend. Another way we can serve someone in a time of need is to speak the truth to them. We all know how our perspective can grow clouded the longer we are in a time of suffering or struggle.

Identify a Christian friend or family member who is going through a tough time. Write them a note to let them know you are praying for them and want to offer any practical help possible. Along with this, write out the words of Romans 8:31–39. Serve them by reminding them of a powerful promise of God. They are not alone today, and they will never be alone. Even in their darkest hours, God is with them. Nothing can change this!

Loving and Being Loved

Jesus calls us to complete and radical devotion. He does not want us pledging our love and allegiance to anyone, or anything, except Him. In Luke 16:13 Jesus says, "No servant can serve two masters. Either he will hate the one and love the other, or he will be devoted to the one and despise the other. You cannot serve both God and Money."

Take time in the coming week to "red tag" at least three or four items around your house that you really like. Make red tags and write the word *temporary* on them and tape them to these items where you can clearly see them. Let this be a reminder that your Savior means infinitely more to you than any of the stuff of this world. Use this as a teachable moment with your kids.

As an added bonus, if anyone asks you what the tags mean, use this opportunity to tell them exactly how much Jesus means to you.

SESSION FIVE

Living in Community

ROMANS 14

Some years ago there was a book published that caught the fancy of the American people. It was called *Real Men Don't Eat Quiche*. Shortly thereafter another book was published entitled *Real Women Don't Pump Gas*. The first one described what "real men" do and don't do and the second one made an effort to clarify what "real women" do and don't do.

Shortly after this I decided to take a stab at this same kind of literature. I wrote a few statements about what real pastors do and don't do. Here are a few examples:

Real pastors don't heat their baptistery.
Real pastors don't wear plaid shorts to the church picnic.
Real pastors don't back down from the choir director.
Real pastors wear a Hard Rock Café T-shirt under their
    clerical gown.

The truth of the matter is, we all have a sense of what real Christians do and don't do. Our perception of what is proper and what is forbidden is often based on our own background. In the denomination where I grew up, a real defining sign of a godly, mature Christian was that you attended Sunday *evening* worship services as well as the morning service. If you showed up to evening services in August, when the church was hot and the air was particularly thick, you were almost considered a saint!

Most Christian groups have an unwritten set of do's and don'ts that everyone knows. They are not often spoken, but almost everyone in their group knows that following these unspoken rules impacts the way others measure your faith.

They might be about clothing fashion, style of music, length of hair, proper forms of recreation, or expressiveness in worship. It can become very easy to make value judgments about who is a mature Christian and who is not based on these extra-biblical externals.

Making the Connection

1. What are some of the unwritten, extra-biblical *do's* in your Christian community that are seen as a sign of spirituality and maturity?

What are some of the don'ts *in your Christian community that might cause others to secretly question your spiritual maturity?*

Knowing and Being Known

Read Romans 14:1–12

Tradition

He is a little man in a long green coat and a cocked hat, standing with one leg on a steep roof, playing the fiddle. He is all of us, trying to make some meaningful music out of our lives but lacking a level place to stand on. "We are all fiddlers on the roof, trying to scratch out a pleasant little tune without falling down and breaking our necks." And how do we keep our balance? "I'll tell you," sings Tevye in the opening song of the musical *Fiddler on the Roof,* "in one word, I'll tell you, tradition! Because of our tradition, everybody knows who he is and what God expects him to do."

—Lewis B. Smedes, *Mere Morality* (Eerdmans, 1983, p. 1)

To know in advance what God expects us to do—before a new wind threatens to blow us off the roof, before a new crisis shakes our foundations—would be a great gift! Is it possible?

As *Fiddler on the Roof* progresses, Tevye has to face the very same issues Paul addresses in the fourteenth chapter of Romans. What is core and central to the faith? What must be held without compromise? And what is simply human tradition that requires a certain level of flexibility? These are questions we must all face.

2. What are some of the examples of *do's* and *don'ts* (14:1–6) that the apostle Paul raises with the Roman church?

What kinds of conflict were these followers of Christ facing?

3. How would you describe the spirit or attitude (14:1–6) Paul was encouraging Christ followers to have toward those who live with a different set of extra-biblical rules than we have?

How might this teaching of Paul change the way you look at those who cross some of the extra-biblical boundaries that are a part of what you believe?

4. What are some of the core biblical beliefs Paul highlights (14:7–12) that we can all affirm?

Why is it essential that we don't flex or compromise on these core beliefs?

5. What will our Christian community look like if we keep our focus on the core, central teachings of the Bible?

What will our Christian community look like if we keep our focus on all of our personal extra-biblical norms, standards, and traditions and impose them on others?

Read Romans 14:13–23

From Foreign to Familiar

When a person first learns to play a musical instrument, the motions are mechanical. Placing fingers on the keys or strings can feel foreign. Keeping the rhythm while reading music and trying to play seems like an impossibility. However, with time and lots of practice, the instrument begins to feel natural to the touch. The music begins to make sense. What was once foreign is now familiar. As musicians mature they grow more and more free to express themselves through their instrument. It is no longer work; it becomes joyous, passionate art!

When young people first take driver's education, everything feels strange. When they sit in the driver's seat and take the wheel into their hands for the first time, it feels unnatural. Everything is by the book. Their hands are at the official ten o'clock and two o'clock position. Before they change lanes they go through the predefined procedure: think, mirror, signal, and blind-spot check. They might even hear the voice of their instructor in their ear when they are driving alone. But it doesn't take long before this mechanical procedure is replaced with a free-flowing lane change. Six months later they have one hand on the wheel, with a burger in the other. They have clearly developed a freer approach to their driving experience.

Although imperfect comparisons, these two illustrations reflect a critical theme in the apostle Paul's teaching. It is immature followers of Christ who stay locked into rigid legalism. It is the "weaker" brothers and sisters who start out their Christian life very mechanically and legalistically, and never get beyond it. They are happy to set out a list of do's and don'ts, keep them religiously, and never discover the joy of freedom in Christ.

6. In this portion of Romans, Paul speaks primarily to stronger Christians about how they should conduct themselves toward weaker or less mature followers of Christ. What is Paul's counsel to mature Christians in relationship to their weaker brothers and sisters?

7. List three or four specific extra-biblical behaviors that could cause tension between members of your church. (This could range from specific behaviors on a Sunday, to drinking a glass of wine, to a style of worship, to any other area of potential tension.)

   •

   •

   •

   •

   If you have a brother or sister who feels deeply convicted about one of the areas listed above, how might you conduct yourself in a way that expresses love and keeps them from stumbling?

8. What is the sacrifice Paul invites us to make for the sake of our brothers and sisters in Christ (14:21)?

   Tell about a time you chose to limit your freedom for the sake of protecting a Christian brother or sister.

9. What is one situation you will face in the coming weeks where you sense you may need to limit what you do for the sake of another believer?

   How can your small group members pray for you and encourage you to express sacrificial love in this relationship?

Celebrating and Being Celebrated

Reflect on the areas of your life where you have experienced freedom through Jesus Christ. Take time as a group to celebrate your freedom and to thank God for breaking the chains of bondage and giving you freedom to walk with joy in Christ.

Serving and Being Served

Reflect on areas of your life where you have a higher level of freedom than some of the followers of Christ around you. Identify any ways you may have been causing others to stumble. Confess this to God. Pray for strength and wisdom so that you will no longer cause a brother or sister to stumble in this area of their personal weakness. Seek to serve them by praying for them to grow more free in this area, as well as committing yourself to do nothing that would cause them to stumble.

Loving and Being Loved

We all come from various traditions. Some people have habits or behaviors that may be very important to them. Whenever possible, we need to honor these traditions and the people who practice them. I am not speaking of legalism or areas of weakness, just traditions that others appreciate. For instance, some people love old hymns played on an organ. Others appreciate praise choruses led by a whole praise team. Both of these are pleasing to God. There is no right or wrong here, no better or worse, no more mature and less mature taste in musical styles.

The problem comes when we insist our way is the best way. Some even claim that their personal likes are God's likes

as well. They put down and criticize what is rich and precious to others.

Seek an opportunity to bless and affirm someone else's tradition or tastes. It might not be your favorite, but let them know that you respect their tradition and thank God for all that it means to them.

Accepting One Another

ROMANS 15

Who could ever forget what happened on the steps of the Lincoln Memorial on August 28, 1963? Martin Luther King, standing in front of a massive and silent multitude, spoke words that have become a part of American history. He said, "I have a dream!" In this speech he outlined the vision for an integrated society, a just society, a compassionate society. His listeners were stirred to the core of their being. Not only did he have a dream, but he inspired others to enter this dream and help change the world.

The apostle Paul was another man with a dream. Like every follower of Christ, he knew the passion and hope that only Jesus Christ could inspire. One of Paul's greatest dreams was to preach the message of Jesus where no person had ever gone before. He wanted to travel into uncharted waters and bring the contagious message of the Christian faith to people who had never heard the name of Jesus.

This dream drove Paul forward every day of his life, helping him to endure imprisonment, beatings, shipwrecks, rejection, hunger, and much more. Paul was willing to pay any price to carry out his God-given dream to plant churches in parts of the world that had never heard the great news of Jesus.

Some people looked at Paul and thought he was out of his mind. How could one man bring the message of Jesus Christ all the way to Rome and then to Spain? This would mean traveling over 1,600 miles (with no planes, trains, or automobiles). In the same way, some people listened to Martin Luther King and mocked his dream. In a day of segregation, racial hatred, and radical prejudice, who could imagine children of different races playing together with no concern for the color of their skin? Let's face it, every big dream will meet with some resistance. But if it is a dream from God, it is always worth pursuing!

Making the Connection

1. What is a dream you believe God has placed on your heart? Use one of the categories below to describe your dream:

   - Concerning your spiritual gifts and how God could use you in His service
   - Concerning God's plan for your family life
   - Concerning how you could leverage your material resources for His purposes
   - Concerning how God could use your church to impact your local community
   - Concerning some other dream God has placed on your heart

2. When we articulate a dream God has placed on our heart, we can get all kinds of responses. Describe a time when someone discouraged you from pursuing a dream. How did this make you feel, and how did this impact your pursuit of the dream?

Reflect back to a time when someone encouraged and inspired you to seek your dream. How did this make you feel, and how did this impact your pursuit of the dream?

Knowing and Being Known

Read Romans 15:1–33

Success or Significance?

A business friend of mine who has had quite an impact on my life said to me one day, "After I got established in my career and started getting the hang of how to do it well, I started asking myself if I was going to spend the rest of my life simply trying to roll up the score." He said, "Once I had the basic needs of my family met and knew how to do my job, I had to ask myself if I wanted to invest the rest of my life simply putting more money in the bank and accumulating more things."

At this critical moment of his life, God awakened him to the deepest dream of his heart. He realized that his life should be invested in serving the church, beautifying the bride of Christ, and advancing the cause of Christ. Since then, he has totally reordered his life. His priorities are radically different. He has shifted his life focus from success to significance.

He still works in the marketplace and is still successful, but his primary life passion is the church of Jesus Christ. He works hard to have integrity in the marketplace, but he pours out his life to further the cause of the church. His greatest passion is to see biblically functioning communities of believers all over the world. This is his dream, and he is pursuing it with all of his strength.

3. If you were to use this chapter as the text of Paul's "I Have a Dream for the Church" speech, what would you say are the primary characteristics that mark a biblically functioning Christian community?

4. Paul's vision of the church is rooted in the truth of the Scriptures (v. 4). What are three specific strengths that the teaching of the Bible bring to the church?

   •

   •

   •

   Why is each of these essential for the health and strength of the church?

Nine One Anothers

In this chapter, Paul gives nine specific qualities of a church that is functioning in a way that is pleasing to God. Each of them touches on how we relate to one another. As members of a biblically functioning Christian community, we will:

1. Bear one another's weaknesses (v. 1).
2. Edify (build up) one another (v. 2).
3. Have a spirit of unity with one another (v. 5).
4. Hunger to worship with one another (v. 6).
5. Accept one another (v. 7).
6. Instruct (challenge) one another (v. 14).
7. Support one another (vv. 26–27).
8. Pray for one another (vv. 30–31).
9. Refresh one another (v. 32).

Paul's dream was for every church that names the name of Christ to have all nine of these characteristics marking their life together.

5. Describe a struggle or time of weakness that a brother or sister is going through right now.

What can you do to help them bear their burden?

6. If Paul could have had every member of the Roman church remember one key message from this letter, it may have been this one: "Accept one another, then, just as Christ accepted you, in order to bring praise to God" (Romans 15:7). What would this verse have said to the Jewish and Gentile Christians who were still focusing on their differences?

Why is this message essential for health in the church today?

7. How did the churches in the first century show tangible support for each other (vv. 23–29)?

  • Jewish Christians to Greek Christians

- Greek Christians to Jewish Christians

- All Christians to each other

What was their attitude and heart condition as they cared for each other?

8. Paul pleaded for the Christians in Rome to uplift him in prayer (vv. 30–32). What were Paul's specific prayer requests?

What do you learn about the importance of praying for one another through Paul's request?

9. Each of us receives encouragement and refreshment in different ways. Describe a time someone did or said something that brought deep refreshment to your heart.

If a friend or small group member wanted to encourage, uplift, or refresh you, what would minister to you?

Celebrating and Being Celebrated

Paul honestly desired to receive refreshment from the Roman church by being with them. God desires to bring health, strength, encouragement, and joy into our lives through other followers of Christ. One way this happens is when we authentically express our appreciation for each other. Take time in prayer as a group to lift up praises to God for each member of your small group.

Serving and Being Served

You spent time in this study telling of various people you know who are carrying heavy burdens in their life right now. You also discussed ways you could share the burden. Identify one of these needs that you could address as a small group. Who is one person you know that is carrying a burden that your small group could help to shoulder? It might mean a one-time act of service or help. It might mean a commitment of regular help over an extended period of time. It could mean taking a collection and giving it directly or anonymously. Pray and let the Holy Spirit lead you to the right person and best way to help bear his or her burden.

Loving and Being Loved

Paul calls us to have a spirit of unity with one another (v. 5). Identify one relationship you have with another follower of Christ that has broken down. Invite your small group members to pray for you in your efforts to restore unity in this relationship. Seek their counsel, support, and wisdom as you make every effort possible to reestablish community with this person. If there is a chance that any of your small group members might know this person, be sure not to use a name. Simply communicate the situation and seek their help as you strive for unity in this relationship.

Session One — An Urgent Message to the World
ROMANS 1

Question 2

Paul was clear that he had been praying faithfully (v. 10) and consistently for an open door to travel to Rome and be with the followers of Christ. We all know that when we pray for something over time, a deep passion and sense of urgency is birthed in our heart. Paul had this deep longing to minister among the Roman Christians (v. 11).

Paul even uses the word *eager* (v. 15) to describe his attitude toward coming to Rome and preaching the Good News of Jesus Christ. Like a child waiting for Christmas morning to arrive, Paul couldn't stand the thought of another day or hour passing until he could finally meet with his brothers and sisters in Rome.

To express his deep conviction, Paul lets the Roman Christians know that he has no shame about the gospel of Jesus Christ. He won't shrink back or withhold anything he can offer. When he finally is able to be with them face-to-face, they will get the full urgency and intensity of his passion for proclaiming this life-changing, power-unleashing message.

The bottom line is clear to see: This is no game for Paul. His call to tell others about what Jesus Christ has done and how to become a fully devoted follower of Christ has consumed his whole life. It defines who he is as a person, permeating his personal life, professional life, and every aspect of who he is. Nothing is more urgent to Paul than this message he is bringing to the Roman church.

Jesus' love for His church is beyond description. Paul walked so closely with Jesus that he learned to love the things Jesus loved. This meant that Paul's heart beat with an extraordinary passion for the church. In the same way, our hearts should

long for the health, strength, and growth of the church. We should love what our Savior loves. First on this list is the church.

Question 3

In verses three and four Paul paints a wonderful picture of Jesus Christ by taking three aspects of the person of Christ and weaving them together. First, Paul tells us that Jesus was a human being, related to King David of the Old Testament. Jesus shares our humanity.

Second, Paul tells us that Jesus was born of the Holy Spirit. Jesus had no human birth father, for He was the Son of God! This truth assures us that He has the power to overcome everything, including sin, death, and the power of the enemy.

Third, to finish this amazing portrait, Paul lifts up the truth that Jesus Christ is Lord. His lordship was confirmed and sealed when He rose from the dead. Jesus broke the power of the grave and rose victorious! Every knee will bow to Him. He is Lord!

Question 4

Paul had heard some wonderful and positive reports about Christ's followers in Rome. He was encouraged by what he had heard, and his heart was warm toward these committed and faithful Christians. Because of all he had heard, his heart hungered to be with them, to meet them face-to-face, and to experience true Christian community with them.

Paul was known, maybe more than any other person in the Bible (except Jesus), for his deep and unwavering love for the church. In the book of Colossians, Paul even communicated that he would be willing to suffer if it would further the cause of the church. If you know the story of Paul's life, you know this is exactly what happened on more than one occasion.

Question 5

Paul is clear that a knowledge of God has been given to all people. This means that everyone is without excuse. There is no person on the face of the globe who is unaware of the reality of God. God has taken care of this by revealing Himself to every man, woman, and child on the face of the globe. The issue is not do they know God exists, but will they accept this reality.

Theologians refer to this as "general revelation," a revealing of the identity and existence of God that is made available to everyone. Paul is saying that creation gives evidence that there is a God who is powerful, creative, brilliant, multifaceted, and all-wise. He is saying that you can't walk this planet and some day claim that there were no clues strewn about the universe that pointed to the existence of God.

If we walk into a parking lot and see a new sports car, we believe that this vehicle has a designer. If we look at the watches on our wrists, we would never think that they came into existence all on their own or by some random act. This makes no sense at all. Yet the heavens and earth are so much more complex than any car or watch. The working of the human body and brain make the most complex automobile look like a child's toy. God has revealed Himself clearly for all to see.

Paul even takes things a step further. He not only argues that we can conclude that God exists through the things He has made, but that through His creation we can know God's eternal power and divine nature. All we have to do is look around and we can see His divinity. God's signature is all over the place!

Question 6

Rejection. This is the core of the crime or sin described by Paul. He states this sin in different ways, but it all comes back to the fact that God has revealed Himself and some have willfully denied His existence and rejected Him. This comes through when we refuse to give God glory or thanks for all He has done. It is seen when we call our foolishness wisdom. It is confirmed when we walk in utter darkness and claim we are walking in the light. It happens when we reject the very One who made the heavens and the earth and everything in them and then bow down and worship toys and trinkets that mean nothing. The core of what Paul is saying is that God has clearly revealed Himself, but many people choose to suppress what He has shown them and reject the Creator.

Questions 8–9

No loving parent would ever give their children over to bad choices and a rebellious lifestyle, would they? Actually, too many could tell their own story of how they hit a point where this is exactly what they had to do.

God, as the perfect heavenly Father, does this as well. There is a point where our rebellion gets so strong that God gives us over to our own desires and passions. The downward spiral begins, and we dive deeper and deeper into sin. What we have to remember is that God never releases a child without tears. And God is always ready to receive us back home as soon as we are ready to return.

Question 10

Sometimes it seems the only intolerable act in our culture today is intolerance. Acceptance is the law of the land. Tolerance is demanded and affirmation of almost anything is seen as an expression of love and kindness. Things have really not changed that much since the apostle Paul lived.

At the bottom of the downward spiral of sin is an acceptance and affirmation of rebellion. People get to the point where they might know some things are wrong, but they look the other way, reject the truth of God, and approve of those who practice these rebellious acts. Paul says when you hit this point, you are seeing the lowest of the low for human beings. Sadly, the words of Paul reflect the climate of our day.

Session Two — How to Find Forgiveness for Moral Failures
ROMANS 3

Question 1

Godly leaders in a church will do all they can to protect a church from even the hint of division. We need to protect and uplift the church of Jesus Christ, never to destroy it. We should pray for the bride of Jesus Christ to be radiant and beautiful, not defaced, marred, and scarred.

It brings so much joy to the Evil One when he can split a church and drive a wedge between followers of Christ. The Enemy is always looking for a way to divide brother from brother and sister from sister. Conflict in the church and tension between brothers and sisters delight the Evil One.

If you read the book of Romans closely, it seems evident that Paul was concerned about the possibility of a split. You see, the church at Rome was made up of two well-defined groups of believers. First, there were those who had a Gentile background. They did not grow up with the heritage of Judaism, but came out of a completely non-Jewish background. Second, there were those who had grown up in the synagogue as practicing Jews. These two groups could easily be at odds with each other.

The Gentile converts came out of a worldly background that often included loose living, pagan worship, and rebellion toward God. The Jews had grown up obeying the Law of God as well as many extra rules and regulations developed by their rabbis over the years. These two groups were often at odds with each other.

There very easily could have been times when the Gentiles would sit on one side of the aisle and the Jews on the other side. The Jews might have looked across the aisle and wondered, "How can God love and accept people with such questionable backgrounds? They might be saved, but those rough-edged Gentiles need a lot of sanctifying if they are going to make it. How can we worship, fellowship, and receive the sacraments with these moral misfits?"

On the other hand, the Gentiles could have looked back across the aisle and thought, "How can those uptight and legalistic Jewish Christians begin to understand God's love and grace?"

Paul knew he had his work cut out for him. God wanted to connect these two very different groups together into one community of faith.

Question 2

Paul spends the second chapter of his letter and the first eight verses of chapter three convincing the Jews that they are sin-

ful before God. Instead of trusting in Christ, the Jewish believers were trusting in law, circumcision, and family lineage. They saw themselves as the preservers of truth and God's favorite people, and they looked down on all those who were not Jews (the Gentiles). This prideful attitude had even infiltrated the church. Now that there were both Jewish Christians and Gentile Christians worshiping in the same congregations, would these attitudes go away? Apparently not! After addressing the Jews (who needed a little more persuading of their sinful condition), Paul turns his attention back to everyone in the church.

Paul says to everyone in the church at Rome, "You have more in common than you might think! There is something that binds you all together and marks every one of your lives. It does not matter if you were born a Jew and have the purest family ancestry imaginable. And it does not matter if you are a Gentile and came from far away from the faith. There is one thing that you all have in common that brings you to exactly the same place of need: You are all sinners."

It is as if Paul is saying, "Stop all the needless bickering and fighting. No more arrogance about your family heritage, and no more being intimidated by those who seem more religious. Cross the center aisle, look each other eye-to-eye, and say, "I'm sorry. I'm a sinner just like you, and I am in desperate need of the Savior."

Question 3

It is our human propensity to dethrone God, or to neutralize God. We like to say that God will smile benignly at some of the things we have done, or judge on a curve. I have even heard people say, "My God will never, ever condemn a human being for occasional moral misfortunes or lapses in judgment." Because our hearts are desperately sinful, we have an amazing ability to deceive even ourselves.

Question 4

As a small group leader, it is important to clarify that the "law" in this passage is not the legal code of our day, but something very specific—the Old Testament commandments. The Law of

God will never save anyone, because no one can follow it perfectly. The law brings us to our knees and makes us profoundly aware of our own sinfulness. This, in turn, should lead us to look for a Savior, someone who can deliver us from the consequences of our sinful lives.

The reality of our sin and the existence of the law, bearing witness to our moral failure, should bring us all to a point where we can admit that we are sinners. We must acknowledge that we will stand without excuse before a holy God. We must realize that if it were not for Jesus Christ, we would receive righteous judgment, which would mean separation from God in hell forever. We have committed cosmic treason, and a holy God can't and won't wink at our sin.

Questions 6–8

In Romans 6, Paul clarifies the cost of our sinful condition and the hope found in Jesus: "For the wages of sin is death, but the gift of God is eternal life in Christ Jesus our Lord" (v. 23). The third chapter of Romans emphasizes the reality that we have all sinned and none of us measures up to God's perfect standard. The just and fair judgment of God on our sins is the death penalty. This punishment must be paid to satisfy God's holy and just nature.

This is why Jesus came for us. He was God in human flesh. He lived a perfect and sinless life, and yet He died to pay the price for our sins. We are all under the death sentence of our own sin. Someone has to pay the penalty. It will be you or Jesus. There is no other way. Paul pleads with us to accept this indescribable gift of salvation through the atoning, sacrificial death of Jesus on the cross.

Questions 9–10

When we realize the source of our salvation, we are changed. Boasting goes out the window! Trying to earn God's favor is a joke—there is no way we can do this on our own merit. Holding petty grudges against other followers of Christ now seems ridiculous. Causing division and conflict in the church is unthinkable. In light of all God has done to extend forgiveness to us, in light of the price He has paid, in light of the

bloodstained cross of Jesus, we begin experiencing transformation. Our attitudes, actions, and motives change.

Session Three — Free at Last
ROMANS 6

Question 1

In the first five chapters of Romans, Paul addresses how a sinner can be made right with God. He is clear that we are all sinners and that God has made a way for us to find forgiveness for our moral failures. First, we need to acknowledge our sinfulness. Next, we need to realize that we can never do enough good works to attain eternal life. This means we have to abandon plan A—an effort to work our way into God's good favor—and we need to adopt Plan B—to receive the free gift that comes to us through Jesus Christ. This is the gift of cleansing us from our sins and of clothing us in the righteousness of Christ. When we do this, we have peace with God, we have access to Him, and we receive His love. When we receive the gift of justification through Christ, everything changes.

Every follower of Christ knows the freedom from bondage that comes through Jesus Christ alone. With this knowledge, we can look at others and see that they are still in slavery to sin. Our hearts break for those we love who believe they are experiencing freedom and life, but who are truly enslaved to sin and heading for eternal death.

Questions 2–4

When we hit chapter six of Romans, we move in a whole new direction. It is like an exit ramp off a highway. We have been heading in one direction, but now we veer off toward a whole new line of thought. We begin to see a whole new landscape of teaching.

From this point on in the letter of Romans, we are not talking about how to be justified (how to come into a relationship with God), but how to be sanctified (how to grow in our relationship with God). Paul shows that when our relationship with God changes, our relationship to sin changes also.

In this sixth chapter of Romans, Paul addresses the truth that not only do people have a sin nature, outside of Christ, but we are sin enthusiasts. People who are slaves of sin can live with moral failures and not even bat an eyelash. They don't even blush. They not only swim in sin, but can splash around and enjoy it! If it feels good, do it. If it sounds good, try it. There is no consideration for God's feelings.

It is important to make a distinction that some people who are still indulging in a sinful life do so in dramatic and shocking ways. Their sins are repulsive to many, and sometimes even to others who don't yet follow Christ. At the same time, there are those whose sins seem a little more tame. Their sins may not be public or deeply offensive to others, but they are still slaves of sin. They may be chronically self-centered. They routinely refuse the promptings of the Holy Spirit, and they say no to God without any guilt whatsoever. They trample the blood of Jesus underfoot and don't even realize they are doing it. They are involved in all kinds of sin, and it feels natural.

Sin enslaves. Those caught in a life of sin are pawns to its power. They are puppets whose strings are being manipulated by the Evil One, and they don't even see it. Deception runs so deep that they believe they are free, but they are not. Their eyes are blinded to their real condition.

Question 5

Paul is reminding followers of Christ that part of the beauty of the believer's baptism is the symbolism of going down into the water laden with sin and bursting forth from the water cleansed and victorious over sin and death. We must never underestimate the significance of the believer's baptism, for it is a graphic demonstration of the death, burial, and resurrection of Jesus, who broke the power of sin and death for all who believe.

Paul says that when Jesus Christ was hanging on the cross, He became the sin sacrifice. The crucifixion of Jesus led to His death; His death led to a burial. In His death, our sins were transferred to Him. When this happened, the condemnation of the holy God was placed on Jesus. When He descended to the grave, He was loaded with our sins. On Easter, when God

resurrected His Son, Jesus burst from the grave glorified, purified, and victorious. He had paid the price of our sins and broken the power of sin and the grave.

Paul says that when we confess our sins and trust in Christ for our salvation, we have, in a symbolic way, gone to the grave with Him and burst forth with Him, changed, purified, and justified. Our enslavement to death and sin has been ended.

Questions 6–7

Paul is clear that transformation happens in the life of a person who has been buried with Christ in His death and risen again to new life. Everything changes. We are now free. We are no longer slaves to sin. This means our motives, actions, words, and life patterns begin to transform. It does not always happen instantaneously, but slowly, over time, God transforms our lives. Where we were slaves and incapable of saying no to sin, we now have the strength to resist. With time we find ourselves saying yes more and more to God and no more and more to the enticements of sin. The very things we used to do that never bothered us now make us uncomfortable. Our desires change. It's a process, but all those who truly experience the freedom that comes through the life, death, and resurrection of Jesus are changed people.

Session Four — It Will Be Worth It All
ROMANS 8

Question 1

The entire Bible is filled with warnings to not get caught up in the stuff of this world. Jesus put it this way: "Do not store up for yourselves treasures on earth, where moth and rust destroy, and where thieves break in and steal. But store up for yourselves treasures in heaven, where moth and rust do not destroy, and where thieves do not break in and steal. For where your treasure is, there your heart will be also" (Matthew 6:19–21).

God wants us to know that some things are eternal and other things are temporary. As followers of Christ, we need to focus on the things that will last forever. We need to be profoundly aware of the seduction that draws us in to loving the things of the world and forgetting the things that really matter.

Question 2

The Enemy is a liar. John tells us, "He was a murderer from the beginning, not holding to the truth, for there is no truth in him. When he lies, he speaks his native language, for he is a liar and the father of lies" (John 8:44). He whispers lies in the ears of Christ followers as often as they will listen. God says, "I forgive you," and the Enemy says, "God could never forgive you." God says, "Nothing could make me stop loving you," and the Enemy whispers, "You have lost the love of God. You crossed the line this time and there is no coming home." We must learn to hear the voice of God and ignore the voice of the Enemy.

Question 3

Paul is crystal clear that Jesus Christ came as the sin offering. A payment for our sin had to be made, and Jesus laid His life down for this express purpose. All of history and all of Paul's teaching hinge on this reality—that through the sacrificial death of Jesus Christ on the cross we are set free from sin and death and given new life. Until we grasp this reality and accept this gift of grace, nothing else will make sense.

Questions 4–6

Paul lays out a clear two-sided reality. In this passage Paul paints a picture of two kinds of people: those who are under the law of the Holy Spirit (followers of Christ) and those who are under the law of sin (nonbelievers). Paul sees a radical difference between these two groups of people.

Those who are under the law of the Spirit have been set free. Their chains are loosed. They are no longer under the condemnation of sin. They no longer have a fear of death. All of the requirements of God's law have been fulfilled for them through the person and work of Jesus Christ. Their patterns of thinking have changed and are continually changing to reflect the Spirit of God. Now their motives and desires grow out of a profound

understanding that they are children of God. A desire to please the Father gives direction to every aspect of their life.

On the other hand, those who are under the law of sin are still in bondage. They might not see it or realize it, but they are shackled to the influences of sin and a future of eternal death. They fall short of God's perfect standard every single day, and have no hope of making things right on their own. Their mind is fixed on whatever their human nature desires, and they invest their time and life pursuing things that will never satisfy or save. They are knowingly devoted to their own passions, wants, and desires.

Questions 7–9

We all face trials, struggles, and suffering in this life. No one will walk through this life untouched by pain. This is a reality we all face at one time or another. However, Paul is clear that the glory God promises is far greater than even the worst sufferings this life can deal us. We need to learn how to keep our eyes fixed on what lies ahead, so that we don't get consumed with the pain of this life.

As a small group leader, when you get to questions seven and eight, encourage small group members to take a few moments of silence to reflect and write down three or four of their sufferings (question seven) or the promises God gives (question eight). From this time of personal reflection and journaling, invite honest discussion.

In these verses, Paul points to many of the promises we have for today and forever. We are set free from our bondage (v. 21). We are children of God (v. 21). We are lovingly adopted (v. 23). We have hope (v. 24). We are saved (v. 24). We receive help in our times of weakness through the presence of the Holy Spirit (v. 26). We have One who intercedes for us, the Holy Spirit (v. 27). We are justified and glorified (v. 30). These are just a sampling of what God has promised to His followers.

Question 10

This passage is one of the most encouraging and uplifting passages in the Bible. Take time as a group to celebrate the radical promises of God. If we grasp this reality, our whole outlook on life changes. We realize that we belong to God—nothing will ever change this!

Session Five — Living in Community
ROMANS 14

Question 1

Back in the years when I was leading youth ministry, I had an opportunity to send a small group of four women leaders for a time of refreshment and retreat on a boat in a harbor in West Michigan. They had been serving tirelessly and needed a break. They were faithful in ministry, mature in faith, and loved the Lord deeply.

When they were on this time away, they got up on Sunday morning and went to a little church affiliated with the denomination I grew up in. I was proud to discover they had actually made attending worship a priority during their time away. I had a casual conversation with a woman from that church who knew me and who was aware these young women were staying near this particular church for a week. This woman told me that she felt these four ladies should not be considered spiritual enough to be leaders in ministry because they had failed to attend worship in both the morning and the evening.

When I had this conversation, everything in my spirit wanted to set that woman straight. I wanted to say, "Come on, take the blinders off! These are some of the most godly women I have ever known. Their commitment to Christ inspires me. Please don't make a sweeping value judgment on their spiritual condition based on your expectation that they attend an evening service, in August, while they are on vacation."

The apostle Paul is concerned about these sorts of things in this chapter of Romans. He is deeply concerned that followers of Christ stop judging each other on outward appearances and human regulations.

Questions 2–3

Paul is teaching that we are part of a very big church made up of many people from diverse backgrounds. There are biblical laws that all of us have to comply with, but there are also all kinds of little extra-biblical taboos and mores that develop over time in a church. These are not essentials and core issues. Don't let them divide you!

Paul addresses some specific areas where the followers of Christ in Rome were experiencing turmoil. They had established extra-biblical regulations about what a person could eat or not eat. They had also added many rules to specify how certain days were to be celebrated. This was particularly true about what could and could not be done on the Sabbath. Paul was calling these people to stop imposing their own standards on others in the Christian fellowship. He was saying, cut each other some slack!

Paul is saying that God has accepted these people—who are you to judge or reject them? Specifically, Paul is saying, you need to accept those people who are rigid, legalistic, and rule-oriented in their faith. When Paul encourages the Romans to accept those who are weak in faith (14:1) he is talking about the legalists who are all caught up in their rules and regulations. These are followers of Christ who are not mature enough to be liberated by the ministry of the Holy Spirit.

Questions 4–5

In this same passage, after Paul has clarified some of the extra-biblical legalism troubling the Roman Christians, he then reminds them of some of the core beliefs that bind them together. In just a few short verses Paul affirms that: we live and die to the Lord (v. 8), Christ died (v. 9), Christ rose (v. 9), Christ is Lord of all (v. 9), we will all stand before God as judge (v. 10), and that every knee will bow before the Lord and every tongue confess His glory (v. 11). If this did not wake up the Romans, what would?

They were arguing over menu items while Paul was bringing them back to the core, crucial issues of faith. We can learn a profound lesson from this. No more fighting over trivialities. Let's focus on our crucified, risen, and living Lord. This will bind us together.

Questions 6–9

I have discovered a sad but recurring reality over my years as a follower of Christ. Many Christians never experience the liberation and freedom God longs for them to have. They are happy keeping a narrow set of rules, often human-made, and never experience the fullness of life in Christ. This is often the case with those who are young in the faith, but sadly, it can be the experience of people who have been in the church for a lifetime.

When we are filled with the Holy Spirit, we no longer need to be a legalistic rule keeper. Our hearts are so fixed on Christ that the thought of walking in rebellion is offensive. However, our freedom does not give us the license to do whatever we want. We need to tune in to those around us. If we are with a weaker brother or sister, we can choose to limit what we do so that we don't tempt them to do something that would damage their faith.

Session Six—Accepting One Another
ROMANS 15

Questions 1–2

I believe God gives dreams to all of His followers. Sometimes these dreams take time to mature, but He gives us all dreams. Romans 15 is a record of a dream God gave Paul, a vision of what the church could be. It is a big dream, and one that some of Paul's colleagues and peers might have laughed at. But it was God's dream, so it became Paul's dream.

As followers of Christ, we need to learn that our dreams can be as big as our God. There will always be critics. And, thankfully, there will also be some who encourage us along the way. We must seek God's calling and dream above the voices of those who would say, "It can't be done!"

Think about Paul at the end of his life. He had followed God's dream and had planted many churches. He had done all

he could to fortify and strengthen these Christian communities. Near the end of his ministry Paul said, "I have fought the good fight, I have finished the race, I have kept the faith" (2 Timothy 4:7). I hope and pray each of us can say this as we draw near the end of our lives.

Question 3

In this one chapter, the apostle Paul lays out some of the primary marks of a biblically functioning community. As a small group leader, you may want to give a few minutes for group members to go back over the passage and take note of the key elements of Paul's vision for the church. We will look at many of these more closely in this study, but allow time for group members to discover these marks of a healthy church on their own.

Question 4

Paul teaches us that the truth of God's Word, the Bible, brings us *endurance, encouragement,* and *hope.* No Christian community will survive without all three of these. A church that cuts loose from its biblical moorings will drift with no vision, no direction, or no hope for the future. Although our churches might look different, our styles of music diverse, and the dress code miles apart, there is one thing we must all have in common: We must be rooted in the Scriptures.

Questions 5–9

We all have one life to live. Paul's teaching on the importance of investing in what really matters should wake us all up to questions of significance. Here's the truth. We will not all be called into a full-time ministry. However, we are all gifted and called to serve. We need to ask, what are we doing with our one and only life? Are our dreams big enough? Are we shooting high enough? Are our visions grand enough?

If we are not absorbed in the advancement of the cause of Jesus Christ on this earth, what are we investing our life in? Are our involvements eternal in nature, or are we entangled in inconsequential activities? We need to look at what makes our heart beat fast. If we are not elbow-deep in the work God is doing in our local church, why not? The local church is God's instrument to change this world. Here are a few brief reflections that might encourage you as you commit yourself to invest your life in the church of Jesus Christ.

1. God longs for us to be a fellowship that bears one another's weaknesses (v. 1). God knows that we have a human tendency to look out for our family and close friends, but that we may avoid those who are hurting or who can bring us down. He hungers to see a church where people lift each other up. We need to get under each other's burdens and lift them together. God hungers to find followers who can joyfully carry each other's burdens.

2. God longs for us to be a church that edifies one another (v. 2). God has a dream for a church where people edify each other. The heart of God is for every single believer to identify his or her spiritual gift and use it to glorify God and serve the other people in the fellowship. God longs for a church where one hundred percent of His people are using their God-given abilities to build up others in the fellowship.

3. God longs for us to be a church where everyone has a spirit of unity with one another (v. 5). Although we may have very diverse backgrounds, we can still have a common mind. God wants us to get along even though we might not always agree. The church should be a place where interpersonal conflict does not go underground or digress into slander. Rather, it should be faced, negotiated, and resolved by the leading of the Holy Spirit.

4. God longs for us to be a church where God's people worship with one another (v. 6). God hungers to find churches where believers are deeply committed to be together for corporate exaltation. His vision is a church where all the believers clear their schedules from one end to the other so that they can come together and adore God.

5. God longs for us to be a church that accepts one another (v. 7). Some argue that this verse reflects the heartbeat of the entire book of Romans. Do you remember how the Jewish Christians and the Gentile Christians were at odds with each other? Some feel the book of Romans is primarily about bringing all these people together to worship the same Lord. Paul

dreamed of a church where every person was accepted and felt it. What a joy that would be!

6. *God longs for us to be a church where brothers and sisters teach one another (v. 14).* God longs to see a church where brothers and sisters are committed to be each other's keepers. We should be jealous of God's reputation and concerned for the spiritual well-being of all the people in the fellowship. God wants us to lovingly and honestly warn, confront, challenge, and rebuke one another. We do this to protect each other from falling into temptation and deception.

7. *God longs for us to be a church where people will support one another (vv. 26–27).* Paul was encouraged by churches who had not only provided for their own needs, but also for the needs of some of the poorer congregations around them. Paul longed for every congregation to have this same commitment and excitement for helping other bodies of Christ. This kind of sharing and support warms the heart of God.

8. *God longs for us to be a church that prays for one another (vv. 30–31).* Paul invited them to uphold him through their prayers. Paul longed to see a church that would pray the power of God into every area of their lives together. The heart of God longs to build churches with believers who pray the power of God into their marriages, child rearing, personal commitment to evangelism, marketplace settings, and every area of life.

9. *God longs for us to be a church that refreshes one another (v. 32).* God wants to pour the refreshment of His living water through us and into the lives of other followers of Christ. This means we need to be a willing conduit for Him to use. What a joy we would experience if every member of a church was willing to be used by God as an instrument of refreshment and blessing to the other members of the church!

This resource was created to serve you.

It is just one of many ministry tools that are part of Willow Creek Resources®, published by the Willow Creek Association (WCA) together with Zondervan Publishing House. Created in 1992, the Willow Creek Association is comprised of more than 4,000 churches, representing some 80 denominations and affiliate offices in 12 countries, that share the values and approaches to evangelism and ministry pioneered by Willow Creek Community Church in South Barrington, Illinois. Its mission is "to inspire, encourage, and equip church leaders around the world to build prevailing churches." Since its inception, the WCA has provided training for tens of thousands of church leaders and volunteers around the world.

Following is a list of ways the Willow Creek Association is linking like-minded leaders with each other and with strategic vision, information, and resources in order to build prevailing churches:

- Conferences—Each year the Willow Creek Association hosts eight conferences at Willow Creek Community Church in South Barrington, Illinois. The conferences, designed to address specific aspects of ministry, host more than 25,000 key church leaders, staff, and volunteers each year:

    Church Leadership Conference (CLC)—"Basic training" in church leadership (two conferences per year)

    Promiseland Conference—for children's ministries, infants to fifth grade

    Student Ministries Conference—for junior and senior high ministries

    The Leadership Summit—for Christian leadership in ministry and the marketplace

Evangelism Conference—for strategic outreach

Small Groups Conference—training on building biblically-based small groups

Arts Conference—teaching on how the arts are vital to the church

- Regional Training Events—The WCA provides training each year in several cities. Designed to motivate, inspire, and train key staff and volunteers on the local church level, these events provide focused training in several key areas—children's ministry, student ministry, money management, evangelism, spiritual formation, the arts, and more—accessible and affordable for anyone to attend.

- Willow Creek Resources®—provides churches with a trusted channel of ministry resources in areas of leadership, evangelism, spiritual gifts, small groups, drama, contemporary music, and more. For more information, call Willow Creek Resources® at 800–876–7335. Outside the U.S. call 610–532–1249, or visit www.willowcreek.org/wca.

- WCA News—a bimonthly newsletter with information on the latest trends, resources, and information on WCA events from churches around the world.

- The Exchange—our classified ads publication to assist churches in recruiting key staff for ministry positions.

- The Church Associates Directory—to keep WCA member churches around the world in touch with each other.

- WillowNet (www.willowcreek.org/wca)—an Internet service that provides access to hundreds of Willow Creek messages, drama scripts, songs, videos, and multimedia suggestions. The system allows users to sort through these elements and download them for a fee.

- Defining Moments—a monthly audio journal for church leaders, in which Lee Strobel asks Bill Hybels and other Christian leaders probing questions to help you discover biblical principles and transferable strategies to help maximize your church's potential.

For conference and membership information please write or call:

The Willow Creek Association
P.O. Box 3188
Barrington, IL 60011–3188
ph: 800-570-9812
fax: 888-933-0035
www.willowcreek.org

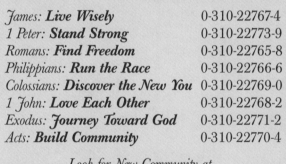

Bring your group to a deeper level of interaction!
InterActions Series
Bill Hybels

Help your small-group members help each other develop into fully devoted followers of Christ. InterActions discussion guides ask for a deeper level of sharing, creating lines of accountability between individuals and moving your group into action. Each book presents six thought-provoking sessions specifically designed to build on the dynamics and interplay of small groups.

Look for Interactions at your local Christian bookstore.

www.willowcreek.org

ZondervanPublishingHouse
Grand Rapids, Michigan 49530
http://www.zondervan.com

Walk with God Together
Walking With God Series
Don Cousins and Judson Poling

This series of six guides (and two leader's guides) provides a solid, biblical program of study for all of the small groups in your church. The Walking With God Series is designed to help lead new and young believers into a deeper personal intimacy with God, while at the same time building a strong foundation in the faith for all believers, regardless of their level of maturity. These guides are also appropriate for individual study. Titles in the series are:

Friendship with God: Developing Intimacy with God	0-310-59143-0
The Incomparable Jesus: Experiencing the Power of Christ	0-310-59153-8
"Follow Me!": Walking with Jesus in Everyday Life	0-310-59163-5
Leader's Guide 1 (covers these first three books)	0-310-59203-8
Discovering Your Church: Becoming Part of God's New Community	0-310-59173-2
Building Your Church: Using Your Gifts, Time, and Resources	0-310-59183-X
Impacting Your World: Becoming a Person of Influence	0-310-59193-7
Leader's Guide 2 (covers these last three books)	0-310-59213-5
Also available: *Walking With God Journal*	0-310-91642-9

Look for the Walking With God Series
at your local Christian bookstore.

www.willowcreek.org

ZondervanPublishingHouse
Grand Rapids, Michigan 49530
http://www.zondervan.com

God's Outrageous Claims

Lee Strobel

Take the Bible seriously and you'll discover that God makes some pretty amazing claims about you—and about what he wants to do in your life. *God's Outrageous Claims* examines important assertions that can transform your life into an adventure of faith, growth, and lasting fulfillment.

Discover how to grow in virtue, relate to others with authenticity, and make a real difference in the midst of a culture that's unraveling at the seams. *God's Outrageous Claims* is your guide to an exciting and challenging spiritual journey that can change you and your world profoundly.

13 Discoveries About
Doubt · Sex · Loneliness · Business · Forgiveness
and More

LEE STROBEL

Author of The Case for Christ

"I work with Lee every day. He not only writes in a compelling manner about God's claims, he lives them out courageously in his own life."

Bill Hybels, senior pastor, Willow Creek Community Church

"Here are practical, workaday helps on the kinds of moral problems faced by believers as well as non-believers. The language is strictly uncomplicated, person-to-person . . . a compassionate book."

D. James Kennedy, Ph.D., senior minister, Coral Ridge Presbyterian Church

Softcover: 0-310-22561-2

Available at your local Christian or college bookstore.

www.willowcreek.org

ZondervanPublishingHouse
Grand Rapids, Michigan 49530
http://www.zondervan.com

The Life You've Always Wanted
John Ortberg
Foreword by Bill Hybels

"John Ortberg takes Jesus' call to abundant living seriously, joyfully, and realistically. He believes human transformation is genuinely possible, and he describes its process in sane and practical ways."

—**Richard Foster,** author, *Celebration of Discipline* and *Prayer: Finding the Heart's True Home*

Willow Creek teaching pastor John Ortberg calls us to the dynamic heartbeat of Christianity—God's power to bring change and growth—and shows us how we can attain it. Salvation without change was unheard-of among Christians of other days, he says, so why has the church today reduced faith to mere spiritual "fire insurance" that omits the best part of being a Christian?

As with a marathon runner, the secret of the Christian life lies not in trying harder, but in training consistently. *The Life You've Always Wanted* outlines seven spiritual disciplines and offers a road map toward true transformation, compelling because it starts out not with ourselves but with the object of our journey—Jesus Christ. Ortberg takes spiritual disciplines out of the monastery and onto Main Street, and leads readers to transformation and true intimacy with God.

Hardcover: 0-310-21214-6
Softcover: 0-310-22699-6

Look for The Life You've Always Wanted *at your local bookstore.*

www.willowcreek.org

ZondervanPublishingHouse
Grand Rapids, Michigan 49530
http://www.zondervan.com

We want to hear from you. Please send your comments about this
book to us in care of the address below. Thank you.

ZondervanPublishingHouse
Grand Rapids, Michigan 49530
http://www.zondervan.com